# After Miss Julie

*After Miss Julie* relocates August Strindberg's *Miss Julie* (1888) English country house in July 1945. In this radical re-of theatre's first 'naturalistic tragedy' the events of Strindberg's original are transposed to the night of the Labour Party's 'landslide' election victory.

**Patrick Marber** was born in London. His first play *Dealer's Choice* premiered at the National Theatre, London in May 1995. It won the Evening Standard Award for Best Comedy and the Writers' Guild Award for Best West End Play. *Closer* premiered at the National Theatre in May 1997 and won the Evening Standard Award for Best Comedy, the Critics' Circle Award and the Laurence Olivier Award for Best Play. *Closer* premiered on Broadway in March 1999 where it won the New York Drama Critics' Circle Award for Best Foreign Play. *Howard Katz* premiered at the National Theatre in June 2001. *The Musicians* will premiere in summer 2004 at the National Theatre Connections Festival.

# After Miss Julie

A version of Strindberg's *Miss Julie*

by

**Patrick Marber**

**Methuen Drama**

Published by Methuen 2003

1 3 5 7 9 10 8 6 4 2

First published in Great Britain in 1996
by Methuen Drama

Re-issued with revisions and a new cover design, 2003.

Methuen Publishing Limited,
215 Vauxhall Bridge Road,
London SW1V 1EJ

Methuen Publishing Limited Reg. No. 3543167

Copyright © 1996, 2003 by Patrick Marber

The author has asserted his moral rights under the Copyright Designs
and Patent Act 1988 to be identified as the author of this work.

A CIP catalogue record for this book is available from the British Library

ISBN 0 413 71150 1

Typeset by SX Composing DTP, Rayleigh, Essex
Printed and bound in Great Britain by
Cox & Wyman Ltd, Reading, Berkshire

**Caution**
All rights in this play are strictly reserved.
Application for performance, etc., should be made to the author's agent:
Judy Daish Associates Ltd, 2 St Charles Place, London W10 6EG. No
performance may be given unless a licence has been obtained.

DONMAR

*For Andrew*

# After Miss Julie

## Note

I wrote *After Miss Julie* in the summer of 1995. It was a commission from Simon Curtis for the BBC 'Performance' series. I was greatly helped by Michael Robinson and Michael Hastings. The former prepared a literal translation from which I worked, the latter was my brilliant script editor at the BBC.

The original cast also suggested new material and various cuts. My grateful thanks to them.

Eight years later Michael Grandage and I worked on the script making a number of changes here and there. Then we did some more work with the cast of the stage premiere. My thanks to him and them.

*After Miss Julie* is not a translation of Strindberg's *Miss Julie*. Rather, it is a 'version' of the original – with all the ambiguity that word might suggest.

I have been unfaithful to the original. But conscious that infidelity might be an act of love.

PM. London. October 2003.

*After Miss Julie* was first broadcast on BBC Television on
4 November 1995, with the following cast:

| | |
|---|---|
| **Miss Julie** | Geraldine Somerville |
| **John** | Phil Daniels |
| **Christine** | Kathy Burke |
| *Music* | Colin Good |
| *Costume* | Jill Taylor |
| *Make Up* | Jean Speak |
| *Sound* | John Relph |
| *Camera* | Peter Woodley |
| *Editor* | Judith Robson |
| *Lighting* | Chris Townsend |
| *Designer* | Sarah Greenwood |
| *Producer* | Fiona Finlay |
| *Director* | Patrick Marber |

The stage premiere was at the Donmar Warehouse, London
on 20 November 2003 with the following cast:

| | |
|---|---|
| **Miss Julie** | Kelly Reilly |
| **John** | Richard Coyle |
| **Christine** | Helen Baxendale |
| *Director* | Michael Grandage |
| *Designer* | Bunny Christie |
| *Lighting* | Neil Austin |
| *Sound* | Matt McKenzie for Autograph |

## Characters

**Miss Julie**, *aged twenty-five*
**John**, *her father's chauffeur / valet, thirty*
**Christine**, *a cook, thirty-five*

## Scene

The kitchen of a large country house outside London.

## Time

26 July 1945. Night and the morning after.

The British Labour Party won their famous 'landslide' election victory on this night.

*The kitchen is a large room on basement level. It's a little gone to seed, neglected. A door leads out to an unseen exterior courtyard and beyond where a dance is in progress. Other doors lead off to the servants' living quarters. In the centre of the room is a large wooden table, chairs at either end, benches at the sides. On the table a pair of black brogues, polish and brushes. Elsewhere a bell and phone system for communication with other areas of the house.*

*Big band dance music from outside continuing throughout the first sequence of the play.*

**Christine** *is alone at a large range, frying kidneys. She is wearing a summer dress with a cooking apron over it.*

*After a while,* **John** *enters. He wears a chauffeur's uniform. He carries a newspaper, the London edition of 'The Evening News'. He puts his car keys in a small cupboard by the door. He goes to the sink and washes his face and hands. Throughout this Christine has stopped working and has been watching him. After a while:*

**John**   Sorry.

**Christine**   It's gone midnight.

**John**   I'm sorry.

**Christine**   I've eaten.

**John**   I had to drive his Lordship to London for the celebrations; big do at Central Hall. Police waved us straight through. You should've seen the crowds.

**Christine**   I heard you park half an hour ago.

**John**   Well, I stopped off at the barn – just to show my face. But then Miss Julie flounces up and says 'Partner me'. I couldn't say no.

*He sits at the table.*

She's off her head, dancing with everyone and anyone, making a right exhibition of herself. She's barking mad, that one.

**Christine**   Don't be rotten. She's lovesick, poor thing.

**John** (*sighs*)   'The Reluctant Officer'.

*Beat.*

D'you reckon it's odd, her staying at home with the servants? I thought she'd go to London with her father.

**Christine**   'Spect she doesn't want to bump into anyone she knows. It's embarrassing for a lady to be jilted like that.

*Pause.*

**John**   I was there. When he gave her the elbow.

**Christine** (*interested*)   Really?

**John**   My natural discretion forbids me to gossip.

**Christine**   Suit yourself.

**John**   They were down at the stables, 'horsing around'. She was mucking about with this whip, 'training him' she said. She was getting him to jump over it, like a dog. He does it twice and each time she gives him a whack. Third time he goes nuts and lashes out with the back of his hand – his ring cut her. Then he takes the whip and breaks it, her heart 'n'all.

**Christine**   And what were *you* doing 'down at the stables'?

**John**   Just . . . idling. Something smells good . . .

**Christine**   Kidneys on toast.

*She serves him the food.*

**John**   You can't beat a kidney – 'specially the black market variety.

*He gives her a playful little smack.*

You might've warmed the plate.

**Christine**   You're worse than his Lordship with your fussing.

*He begins to eat. She strokes his hair and kisses his neck.*

**John**    Don't confuse my appetites.

*She strokes his cheek.*

**Christine**    Bit rough . . .

**John**    My razor's broken. Will you get us a new one?

**Christine**    Anything for his Lordship.

**John**    You can have a lend.

**Christine**    Don't be rude.

*She puts a bottle of beer on the table for him.*

**John**    Beer?! We're supposed to be celebrating.

*He fetches an already opened bottle of red wine.*

His Lordship's best Burgundy. Off the table last night.

**Christine** *hands him a straight glass.*

**John**    *Wine* glass . . .

**Christine**    Isn't he particular? Heaven help the woman who marries you.

*She hands him a wine glass.*

**John**    Easy, you're talking to a gentleman here. *Your* gentleman, perhaps.

*He tastes the wine ostentatiously to amuse her.*

Like Winston Churchill: robust, full-bodied . . .

*He drains the glass.*

And finished.

**Christine**    Poor Winston.

**John**    Hardly *poor*.

*She puts a pan on the stove and begins to stir.*

I remember buying crates of this, with his Lordship, before the war . . .

*Pause. John continues to eat and read his newspaper.*

*After a while he detects the smell from* **Christine***'s pan, it disturbs him.*

What's the stench?

**Christine**    A magic potion. Miss Julie wants it for Emily.

**John**    Cooking for her mutt? You're s'posed to have the night off. (*ironic*) 'It's a scandal!'

**Christine**    Poor dog's up the duff, gatekeeper's pug gave it a seeing to. Miss Julie's livid.

**John**    So what's with the brew?

*She mimes that the potion will induce a miscarriage.*

No!

**Christine**    Honest! She says the dog's betrayed her.

**John**    She's off her rocker!

*He hands her his plate.*

Thanks, love. (*mocking*) The aristocracy just *adore* the animals. That's why they hunt them, we kill what we love.

*He starts to polish the shoes.*

Her mother was a madwoman too. D'you remember her sitting in here? What did she call it – 'fraternising with the troops.' (*shaking his head*) No wonder they're a dying breed. Miss Julie's supposed to be the lady of the house but you should've seen her in the barn gallivanting with the gardeners, even the stable lads got their turn.

**Christine**    And the chauffeur.

**John**    That's different, I'm –

**Christine**    What?

**John**   Just different. The rich should never sell themselves cheap. They try to act common they become common. She dances well though, I'll give her that.

**Christine**   That's not all you'll give her.

**John**   Oi! Respect for your betters, girl! She's a fine-looking filly though. Good skin . . . and . . . et cetera.

**Christine**   You'd be surprised, Claire dresses her and she told me –

**John**   Ah, the jealousy of women.

*A number finishes outside. Applause.*

**Christine**   Will you dance with me when I've done this?

**John**   'Course.

**Christine**   Promise?

**John**   I just said I would.

**Miss Julie** *enters and stands in the doorway. She is flushed from dancing and a little too much alcohol.*

**John** *conceals the wine bottle and rises respectfully, slipping on his jacket and standing almost to attention.* **Christine** *stands by the stove, likewise.*

*Pause.*

**Julie**   Good evening, John. Again.

**John**   Good Evening, Miss Julie.

**Julie**   Is it ready, Christine?

**Christine**   Nearly, Miss.

**Julie**   Will you be an angel and pour it into a bottle?

**Christine**   Yes, Miss Julie.

**Miss Julie** *enters and wanders around.* **John** *and* **Christine** *remain stationary.*

**Julie**  Are you both overcome with excitement?

*They don't know what she means.*

The election!

**Christine**  Yes, Miss.

**Julie**  I take it you did both vote for The Labour Party?

**Christine**  Yes, Miss Julie.

*She continues with her work at the stove.*

**Julie**  And you, John?

**John**  Secret ballot, Miss, I'm afraid I can't reveal.

*She flips him in the face with her handkerchief.*

**Julie**  Impertinence!

**John** (*breathes in*)  Violet.

**Julie**  Sense of smell *and* rhythm, where does his talent end?

*She offers her arm.*

Shall we?

*Pause.*

**John**  No offence meant, Miss Julie, but I did promise this one with Christine.

**Miss Julie** *is disappointed but tries not to show it.*

**Julie**  *To* Christine. She can dance with you any time – can't you, Christine? I command you to lend me this man!

**Christine**  It's fine, I've got to finish this. (*Urges him.*) Go on, John . . .

**John**  I don't mean to be rude but is it proper for you to dance twice in one night with me? People will talk.

**Julie**  Talk? What people? What 'talk'?

**John**   I'm not sure you should favour one member of the staff as opposed to another.

**Julie**   You're doing *me* the favour. I can dance with who I like as often as I like whenever I like. We're a free country now, John. I know, you're a secret Tory, aren't you? Everyone in their place forever.

**John**   No, Miss Julie.

**Julie**   And stop calling me 'Miss'.

*She hits him with her handkerchief again.*

Just for tonight? We can go back to the dark ages tomorrow if you'd prefer. Come on, dance with me! I like the way you lead. All the other men are positively club-footed.

**John**   As you wish, I'm at your service.

**Julie**   It's not an order, it's an invitation! Erase that face of feudal anxiety and come and dance!

*She leads him outside.*

*The music strikes up.*

**Christine** *washes up* **John***'s plate.*

*She puts the wine bottle away.*

*She puts the 'potion' bottle on the table ready for* **Miss Julie***.*

*She removes her apron and hangs it on a hook by her desk.*

**John***'s suit is hanging up, she removes a speck of dust from it and lays it ready for him on the table.*

*She notices that* **Miss Julie** *has left her handkerchief and bag. She carefully folds the handkerchief and places it with the bag next to the potion bottle.*

*She sits at her desk, tired. She yawns, stretches a little. Then she takes a hand mirror and make-up from a drawer and applies lipstick and powder.*

*She looks at herself. Lights a cigarette, smokes, closes her eyes, exhausted.*

*She listens to the music. Waiting for* **John** *to return.*

*She eases back in her chair, trying to get comfortable. She rests her head on her arms on the desk.*

*Her cigarette smoulders in the ashtray. She falls asleep.*

*After a while the number ends. Applause.*

*Presently,* **John** *enters.*

*He sees that she's asleep and gently stubs out the cigarette.*

*He goes to the sink and washes his face. It is a hot night and he is sweating from dancing.*

**Christine** *wakes up, watches him.*

**John**    She's mad all right. Everyone was laughing at her. She was cavorting like a woman possessed!

**Christine**    Don't be mean, she's not herself. She's got the curse this week, Claire told me.

**John** *laughs. A new number strikes up.*

This one's mine.

*She puts her arms round his neck and they begin to sway to the distant music. Their faces are close.*

**John**    You're not angry with me, for going off?

**Christine**    You had to. I know my place and I think that you do too.

**John**    You are going to make a – very – good – wife.

*On each word he kisses her. They are locked in embrace as* **Miss Julie** *enters.* **Christine** *has her back to* **Miss Julie**. **John** *faces her. They stare at each other. Then he gently disengages himself.*

**Julie**    Please, carry on . . .

**Christine**    The medicine's ready, Miss, for Emily.

**Julie**   So I see. (*To* **John**.) You're a charming partner,
running away from your lady like that.

**John**   On the contrary, Miss, I've run *to* her.

**Julie**   Hold on tight to this one, Christine. He's an
incomparable dancer but slippery.

*Pause. She comes further into the room.*

(*To* **John**.) Why are you wearing your uniform? Take it off,
you're not working tonight.

**John**   I haven't had time to change, Miss Julie, I drove
your father up to town.

**Julie**   I know. Is this your suit?

**John**   Yes.

**Julie**   Put it on, it's nice.

*He hesitates. She issues an order, slowly, seductively.*

Put it on, John.

**John**   Will you excuse me, my Lady?

**Julie**   Don't mind me, I'll cover my eyes.

**John** and **Christine** *are shocked and a little embarrassed.*

**John**   With your permission I'll go to my room, Miss.

**Julie**   As you wish.

*He exits with his suit. Pause.*
**Miss Julie** *takes out her cigarette case from her clutch bag.*

**Christine**   Here you are, Miss.

*She gives* **Miss Julie** *a light.*

**Julie**   Thank you. Would you like one?

**Christine**   No thank you, Miss.

*Pause.*

**Julie**   Don't mind me if you have work to do.

**Christine**   Thank you, Miss.

**Christine** *sits at her desk and goes through some paperwork. Pause.*

**Julie**   Is John your fiancé? You seem quite . . . intimate?

**Christine**   We were going to marry but then the war came and . . . we're not engaged officially.

**Julie**   Officially?

**Christine**   Well, I don't have a ring, Miss.

*Pause.*

**Julie** (*to herself*)   I had a ring . . .

**Christine** *stifles a yawn.*

**Julie**   I'm sorry, Christine, am I boring you?

**Christine**   No, Miss Julie, I'm very sorry, I'm tired.

**Julie**   Then you must go to bed.

**Christine**   John promised me a dance, I'll just –

**Julie**   Men like to keep their women, not their promises.

**Miss Julie** *smokes. After a while* **John** *returns in his suit. During the next sequence of dialogue* **Christine** *falls asleep again.*

**Julie**   *Très gentil, Monsieur Jean, très gentil.*

**John**   *Vous voulez plaisanter, Mademoiselle.*

**Julie**   *Et vous voulez parler français.* Where did you learn that?

**John**   I picked up a bit during the war, in France.

**Julie**   I hope that's all you picked up in France.

*The joke falls flat.*

You look quite the gentleman in that suit. *Charmant.*

**John**   You flatter me.

**Julie**    Flatter you?

**John**    My position forbids me to believe that you would pay me an authentic compliment and therefore I must assume that you were exaggerating your praise . . . or flattering.

**Julie**    My, what language! Are you a patron of the theatre?

**John**    I used to accompany your father sometimes. And on his travels abroad too.

**Julie**    But you grew up here, didn't you?

**John**    My father was a labourer on the estate. Our family's worked here for centuries.

*Pause.*

I remember you as a child . . .

**Julie**    Really? What do you remember?

*He nods to* **Christine** *who is now asleep.*

**Julie** (*whispering*)    She's asleep . . .

*They watch her.*

Do you think she snores?

*Pause.*

**John**    No.

*Pause.*

She talks.

*They look at each other.* **Miss Julie** *nervously reaches for another cigarette.*

**Julie**    Smoke?

**John**    No, thank you.

**Julie**    Do you have a light?

*He quietly takes* **Christine**'s *matches from her desk and lights* **Miss Julie**'s *cigarette.*

Merci, Monsieur. Why don't you smoke? I thought all soldiers smoked?

**John**   I'm not a soldier anymore.

**Julie**   You have a weak chest. Yes, my father told me. You were demobbed two months early . . . for your weak chest.

**John**   Yes.

**Julie**   Why don't you sit down?

**John**   I wouldn't take such a liberty in your presence.

**Julie**   But if I ordered you?

**John**   Then I'd obey.

**Julie**   Then sit.

*As he is about to sit.*

No, wait, have you anything to drink?

**John**   Only beer.

**Julie**   'Only'? I like beer. I'm just a simple country girl, John.

*He fetches a bottle of beer and pours her a glass.*

**Julie**   What was the war like?

**John**   Like? Like nothing.

**Julie**   Did you kill lots of Germans?

**John**   Hundreds.

**Julie**   Not thousands?

**John**   Hundreds of thousands.

*He serves her the glass of beer.*

**Julie**   Thank you. Won't you keep me company?

**John**    I'm not really a beer drinker but if my Ladyship commands . . .

**Julie**    Courtesy commands, John.

*As he pours himself a glass she lies back on a bench.*

Do you think I'm a dreadful lush?

**John**    No, my Lady.

**Julie**    *I* think I'm a dreadful lush. Now, a toast . . . to me.

**John**    To you.

**Julie**    To you.

**John**    To me.

**Julie**    To Socialism.

**John**    To Socialism.

**Julie**    To peace.

**John**    To peace.

**Julie**    What else? To Love.

**John**    To Love.

**Julie**    To the workers.

**John**    The workers.

**Julie**    Bravo.

*They drink.*

Now kiss my shoe.

*He stares at her.*

As a sign of respect.

*She dangles her foot.*

*Pause.*

*He moves to her, she snatches her foot away.*

*Pause. They look at each other.*

*She dangles her foot. He moves to her. She snatches it away.*

*He stares at her. She dangles her foot. He moves very fast, catches it, holds it.*

*They look at each other.*

*He kneels and kisses her shoe.*

Very good. Too quick for me, Monsieur Jean.

*He straightens up.*

**John**    I think we'd better drink up, Miss Julie. Someone might see us.

**Julie**    Close the shutters.

**John**    Everyone was talking out there before . . .

**Julie**    What were they saying?

**John**    They were being . . . suggestive. You know what I mean, you're not a child. If they see you in here at night, drinking, alone . . .

**Julie**    We're not alone, your wife-to-be is with us.

**John**    Asleep.

**Julie**    Then I'll wake her.

*She looks at him and then saunters over to* **Christine**.

Christine! Christine!

(*To* **John**.) Dead to the world . . .

Christine! Wake up! Protect us from gossip!

**John** (*sharp*)    Leave her alone.

**Miss Julie** *turns to him, a little shocked by his tone but pleased he prevented her from waking* **Christine**.

**John**    She's been working all day, she's exhausted. Let her sleep.

**Julie**    A noble sentiment, it does you credit.

*She faces him.*

Come outside and pick some lilacs for me.

**John**    I can't. It's not possible.

**Julie**    Why?

**John**    Them.

*He gestures outside.*

**Julie**    They think I could fall for a servant?

**John**    They know no better.

**Julie**    You're a snob! I have a higher opinion of 'them' than you. Come.

**John**    You're welcome to your opinions. I know these people. They don't see what's there, they see what's in their heads.

**Julie**    Well, let's find out. *Come.*

*She faces him, hands outstretched.*

**John** (*softly*)    You're strange . . .

**Julie**    Everything's strange . . . life . . . people . . . everything's a scum that drifts across the water until it sinks.

*Pause.*

Come with me. What does it matter what people say or think?

*He thinks. Moves towards her. He stops, rubs his eye.*

**Julie**    What's wrong?

**John**    Nothing, dust.

**Julie**    Let me see.

*She sits him down and tilts his head back. She gently pushes his eyelid up to look.*

**Christine** *has awoken but is still sleepy . . .*

Keep still . . . don't flinch . . . I can feel you flinching . . .
keep . . . still . . . it's a lash . . . a long black lash . . .

**Christine**   What's the matter?

**John**   Nothing, just a lash.

**Christine**   He's squeamish about his eyes. May I, Miss?

**Miss Julie** *moves to one side.*

**John**   I'm fine, it's gone.

**Christine**   Let me look.

**John**   It's gone.

*Pause.*

**Christine**   You left your bag, Miss, and the medicine's
there for Emily.

**Julie**   Thank you.

*Pause.* **Miss Julie** *shows no sign of leaving.*

**Christine**   Do you need me for anything, Miss?

**Julie**   No, I'm fine. Thank you, Christine.

**Christine**   Then if you'll excuse me, I'll go to bed, Miss.

**Julie**   Of course.

**Christine**   Goodnight, Miss Julie.

**Julie**   Goodnight, Christine.

**John**   Goodnight.

**Christine** *hovers, a little awkwardly.*

**Christine**   Shall I get you up, for church?

**John**   Thank you.

**Christine**   Goodnight, Miss.

**Christine** *exits.* **John** *busies himself, tidying up.*

**Julie**   Where were we?

**John**   You were telling me your theory of life.

**Julie**   Don't be cruel.

*Silence. They become conscious of the music outside.*

**Julie**   Tell me about your visits to the theatre, with my father.

**John**   There's not much to tell. I used to drive him to the theatre, he would sit in the royal circle, I in the Gods. After the performance he would dine at his club, I would wait in the car.

**Julie**   What would you do, 'in the car'?

**John**   Read the paper, the programme, talk to the other chauffeurs . . . in their cars.

**Julie**   Never any women?

**John**   Women chauffeurs? Hardly.

**Julie**   Did you talk to any women? Prostitutes?

**John**   No.

**Julie**   Did my father talk to any women?

**John**   No.

**Julie**   Pros–

**John**   No.

**Julie**   My mother died ten years ago, what's a man to do?

**John**   What indeed.

**Julie**   Do I shock you?

**John**   Not as much as you'd like to.

**Julie**   And would you discuss the play on the way home?

**John**   Sometimes.

**Julie**   Are those his shoes?

**John**   Yes.

**Julie**   Do you like my father?

**John**   Yes.

**Julie**   But do you respect him?

**John**   Yes.

**Julie**   Do you wish he were *your* father?

*Silence. They are close.*

I'm sorry, that wasn't a very grown-up question.

**John**   You're only young . . .

**Julie**   And so innocent . . .

**John**   I think not . . .

**Julie**   It's true . . . Monsieur Jean . . .

*She gazes at him.*

*He moves to kiss her.*

*She slaps him hard on the cheek.*

*Pause.*

**John**   I have work to do, it's way past your bedtime, I suggest you retire.

**Julie** (*amused*)   What work?

**John** *starts polishing a shoe.*

**Julie**   Put it down.

*He ignores her.*

PUT IT DOWN!

*He puts the shoe down.*

You're *proud*. You're a Don Juan – a Don John. Have you ever been to the opera?

**John**    No.

**Julie**    The next time I go to Covent Garden I will take you. But unlike my hypocrite father you will sit with me in the royal circle. Would you like that?

**John**    I have to clean these shoes for the morning. It's not my job to amuse you.

**Julie**    Please don't sulk.

*Silence.*

Well, goodnight then.

*She stubs out her cigarette, leaves her clutch bag on the table and heads for the door. She hovers there.*

*Pause.*

**John**    You've forgotten your bag.

**Julie**    Well, bring it to me then.

**John** *rises and hands her the bag.*

**Julie**    Thank you, John. Goodnight.

**John**    Goodnight, Miss Julie.

*They face each other.*

*Silence. She heads back into the room.*

**Julie**    Do you love Christine very much?

**John**    Of course.

**Julie**    But are you *in* love with her, there's a difference isn't there? I'm not sure I've ever been in love. What about you? Have you ever been in love, John? Sick with love?

*Pause.*

**John**    Only as a child.

**Julie**   Who was she?

*Pause.*

**John**   You know who.

*He looks down.*

Ridiculous, isn't it?

**Julie**   No. Tell me . . .

**John**   I'd been in your father's orchard . . . his 'Garden of Eden' . . . I'd decided to steal some apples . . .

**Julie**   Scrumping.

**John**   Stealing. I was with my mother, weeding your onion beds, in the field out where the barn is now.

**Julie**   I thought the barn was always there?

**John**   No, it was built when you were seven. Those who work the land know it better than those who own it.

**Julie**   You're a red!

**John**   Far from it.

**Julie**   A cynic then.

**John**   Realist. It was the summer of '27 . . . I was twelve . . . I left my mother to it, thought I'd sneak into the orchard and go 'scrumping'. I climbed a tree, dropped down and found myself in a garden party – uninvited – everyone in their finery – your mother – it was a summer evening, like tonight . . . I was in rags – I was scared so I ran and I fell in the slurry pit, I got covered in shit (sorry) – and I ran and ran 'til I ended up on the other side of the lake facing the stables where it's boarded up now . . .

**Julie**   I know.

**John**   And I saw a white dress with a pink ribbon . . .

**Julie**   Here . . .

*She gestures to her throat.*

**John**    Yes. And the girl in the white dress was patting a black pony. I lay in the brambles, I couldn't move or they'd cut me and I watched the girl stroking the animal and I could see the girl was whispering to it, whispering all her secrets. And she looked sad and alone. And I fell in love with you.

**Julie**    I wasn't sad, I was happy. I wanted to die.

**John**    Why?

**Julie**    Because I was so happy.

**John**    But that's not when it started. When I was five . . . I saw your mother pushing you in your pram . . . a blue black pram . . . your carriage. I was five and could already feel the difference between us. My first memory is *you* . . . and a feeling without the words to describe it. Now I can call it love . . . or envy. A man of my class can rise, like bread, but not cake.

**Julie**    But the world is changing . . .

**John**    Not biology.

**Julie**    But there are such opportunities now, for self-improvement . . .

**John**    I'm a self made man if that's what you mean. Your father's been good to me, lending me books. You can learn a lot by observation.

**Julie**    And do you still observe *me*? What do you see?

**John**    Just things. You can be quite a coarse young lady, can't you?

**Julie**    Whatever do you mean?

**John**    Maybe we're not so different; you, me, Christine . . . your officer friend.

**Julie**    *We* never slept together.

**John**   No, but you wanted to.

**Julie**   Nonsense. He wanted to, I refused.

**John**   That's not what I heard . . . and saw.

*Pause.*

**Julie**   When?

**John**   Two weeks ago, the stables.

**Julie**   What a little Peeping John you are. I could have you dismissed for spying on me. I could tell my father and –

**John**   I would have to tell him what I saw: his daughter on her knees unbuttoning the officer's britches.

**Julie**   Nothing happened.

**John**   I know, you scared him off. God knows why they decorated *him* for bravery – probably went to the right school.

**Julie** ( *furious* )   That's enough, this conversation is over.

*She heads for the door.*

**John**   Fine, have I your permission to go to bed?

**Julie**   With Christine?

**John**   Who knows?

*Pause.*

**Julie**   Where are the keys to the boathouse?

**John**   Over there.

**Julie**   Row me out to the lake, I want to see the moon.

**John**   Look out the window.

*Pause.*

**Julie** (*realises*)   You're afraid for *your* reputation.

**John**   Maybe. If anyone suspected I'd be dismissed without a reference, just as I'm getting on. I also have a duty to Christine.

**Julie**   Ah, Christine!

**John**   And you – and your father who trusts me. You play with fire, Miss Julie.

**Julie**   Lucky I'm insured.

*The last number ends outside. Applause.*

**John**   You're tired and drunk, it makes you rash. You'd regret everything in the morning.

**Julie**   Regret what?

**John**   Don't play the innocent.

**Julie**   I *am* innocent, I told you . . . I'm not –

**John**   Go to bed.

*Sound of a drunken crowd approaching from outside.*

Go now, they're coming!

*He quickly extinguishes the lights. He bolts the door and closes the shutters.*

*The crowd are outside the kitchen. Loud.*

*The room is now lit by a single remaining lamp.*

Please, Miss Julie, obey me this once, go now!

**Julie**   Me? Obey you?

**John**   Yes.

**Julie**   And if I don't?

*The sound outside intensifies, the room seems to be surrounded.*

**Julie**   No way out!

*Someone tries the lock. The crowd are singing now.* **Miss Julie** *and* **John** *huddle together.*

**Julie**   Don't be scared. What are they singing?

**John**   An obscene song about you and me.

**Julie**   They wouldn't dare.

**John**   You think they respect you? They're drunk, they're a rabble, they laugh at you, to them you're . . . just . . . mad.

**Julie**   But I'm *nice* to everyone.

**John**   You think you're being nice but you're being patronising. You can't help it, it's in your blood.

*They kiss and begin to struggle with each other's clothes – aggressive, laughing, scared.*

**Julie**   Take me to your room.

*She whispers, intimately.*

**John**   What?

**Julie**   Just take me to your room.

*The banging on the doors and windows increases.*

**John** *and* **Miss Julie** *exit hurriedly.*

*Fade.*

*Later. About five in the morning, grey half-light.*

*The single lamp remains lit. The shutters are closed.*

**Christine** *enters doing up her dressing gown.*

*She heads to her desk, finds a cigarette and lights it. She smokes. She pockets her pack of cigarettes.*

*She goes to the sink and has a sip of water.*

*She looks for an ashtray and finds one on the table. She stares at it.*

*She sees the beer glasses, one with lipstick on the rim.*

*She sees* **Miss Julie**'s *bag and the potion bottle are still on the table.*

*She thinks, takes a drag, leaves her cigarette smouldering in the ashtray.*

*She exits in the direction of* **John**'s *room.*

*Thirty seconds.*

**Christine** *comes back, distraught.*

*She heads back towards her room. Remembers. Returns and picks up her cigarette, takes a drag, stubs it out, unfinished.*

*She exits.*

*Fade.*

*Later. Dawn. Morning light through the cracks in the shutters.*

**Miss Julie** *enters, hair down, smeared make-up, tired. She carries her shoes.*

*She goes to her cigarette case on the table but it is empty.*

*She goes to the sink, washes her face, drinks from her hands.*

*There is a small patch of blood on her dress. She takes a rag and rubs at the dress.*

**John** *enters in trousers and loose shirt, no shoes. He watches her. She sees him, holds up the bloodied rag.*

**Julie**    Where . . . ?

**John**    Here . . .

*He sees the blood on the rag.*

**Julie**    Sorry.

*He takes the rag and puts it in the bin.*

**John**    You all right?

*She nods. They kiss, tenderly.*

*Silence. Exchange of looks.*

**John**    You're all right?

**Julie**    Mmmhm.

*He offers her a chair, she sits.*

**Julie**   Are there any cigarettes around?

**John** *searches* **Christine**'s *desk.*

**John**   'Fraid not.

**Miss Julie** *spots a half-smoked butt in the ashtray. She extracts it happily.* **John** *grins and fetches her a light. She strokes his hand as he offers the flame.*

**Julie**   *Merci, ma chérie.*

**John**   *Mon plaisir.*

*He sits with her as she smokes.*

So . . . New York. That's the place for us. Yeah? New life, new people. I met some GI's during the war, I got their addresses, everything. They live in . . . the Bronx. We'll have to look them up. Maybe they'll help us with the night-club? I imagine it'll be very English, glamorous, sophisticated. They love us over there, they die for the accent. I'll do the books, the bar . . . you'll be front of house, charm everyone . . .

**Miss Julie** *nods, smiles.*

Have to hurry though, Christine'll be up soon and your father's due back. I'll drive us to the station, we'll catch the train, on the boat . . . we're there. How long does it take? Two, three days?

**Julie**   A week.

**John**   A week.

**Julie**   Tell me you love me.

**John**   I love you.

**Julie**   Come here.

*He kisses her.*

**John**   We have to go, Miss Julie.

**Julie**   How can you call me *Miss* now?!

**John**    Because we're *here* . . . in this house with your father's shoes waiting to be cleaned. And me sitting here full of respect . . . that bell rings – I jump. But in America it'll be different . . . I won't feel suffocated . . . I'll be rich.

**Julie**    I don't care if you're rich. Tell me you love me.

**John**    I love you.

*They kiss.*

Come on, be practical. New York, the nightclub, what do you think?

**Julie**    It sounds fine but a business requires capital, do you have any?

**John**    Of course: experience, expertise, nous – that's capital of a sort.

**Julie**    It won't buy you a railway ticket.

**John**    So . . . we need a backer . . .

*Pause.*

**Julie**    John, I don't have any money. I don't have a bean. It's all in . . . trust.

*Long silence.*

**John**    Oh well . . .

**Julie**    What . . . ?

**John**    We stay here.

**Julie**    I can't stay here . . . as your mistress. My father – people – we can't stay here, surely you see that?

**John** (*cold*)    I don't see anything.

**Julie**    But we won't need money, we'll be together.

**John**    We need money to *be* together.

*Silence.*

**Julie**   What have I done?

**John**   Fallen . . . briefly . . . but pleasurably, I trust.

**Julie**   You hate me . . . ?

**John**   No.

**Julie**   You took advantage of me?

**John**   Vice versa, I think.

**Julie**   But you just said you loved me . . . ?

**John**   You confuse love and desire.

**Julie**   I love *you*.

**John**   Congratulations.

**Julie**   How can you . . . what *are* you?

**John**   Just a man. Stop acting the weeping debutante, Miss Julie. We had a roll in the hay, forget it, have a drink, you're more fun when you're tight.

**Julie**   You owe me respect at least.

**John**   That's the last thing you wanted in there. Do you know, you actually shocked me.

**Julie**   You're disgusting.

**John**   No, *you're* disgusting. I told you it would end in tears. I have work to do.

*He starts polishing the shoes.*

Isn't this where we started?

**Julie**   But the things you said . . . ? What about your story? The white dress, the pony . . . ?

**John**   I told you what you wanted to hear, it's called seduction.

**Julie**   Am I your conquest? Nothing more?

**John**   Don't force me to be cruel.

**Julie**   Tell me what I am.

*Pause.*

**John**   A fuck.

**Julie** (*childlike, to herself*)   I'm all dirty.

**John**   So wash.

**Julie**   STAND UP WHEN YOU SPEAK TO ME!
STAND UP! REMEMBER YOUR POSITION!

*He stands.*

**John**   Which one, Madame? There were so many.

**Julie**   You're still a servant, you scared little squaddie,
you're still a servant.

**John**   And you're a servant's slut. Don't come on all
superior with me, Miss Julie. No woman of my class would
accost me the way you did last night, no woman of my class
would want what you wanted last night; sweating and
braying, your face in the pillow, biting your hand to stop
yourself screaming the house down. You'd shame a two-bit
tart in Piccadilly.

**Julie**   Do I deserve this?

**John**   What's a man to think if you beg him to beat you?

*She breaks down.*

**Julie**   Please no more . . . I know . . . I deserve this . . . I'm
bad . . . I'm a bad girl.

*He puts his arms round her, full of pity and desire.*

**John**   No you're not . . . I'm as much to blame . . . I didn't
mean what I said . . . please, I'm sorry . . .

**Julie**   Hurt me again.

**John**   You mustn't say that, things just . . . went too far.
No one knows, you must try to forget about it.

**Julie**   Did you love me? At least in bed?

**John**   Of course I did, couldn't you tell?

**Julie**   How could I? I have no experience, I haven't lived.

**John**   Come on, you're being –

**Julie**   DON'T TELL ME WHAT I'M BEING!

*Beat.*

Do I look ugly?

**John**   You're not at your best.

**Julie**   Is this what you wanted? Me – reduced? Is this your revenge? Your little class victory?

**John**   No. I've dreamt about you all my life . . . and now I have to wake up. I'm not saying I couldn't love you, of course I could . . . I only have to look at you . . . you're gorgeous.

*He tries to kiss her.*

**Julie**   Get off! GET YOUR HANDS OFF ME! What kind of a man is excited by a woman's despair?

**John**   Any man, I imagine.

*She paces round the kitchen, almost oblivious to him.*

**Julie**   I must run away. I can't stay here, I could never live it down and when my father finds out he'll kill me. He plays the Labour peer but he despises the lower classes, they're too stupid and disappointing. He'd sack you on the spot and make my life a misery. And I won't be a laughing stock for the servants – you say they find me condescending?

**John**   Patronising.

**Julie**   Shut up, I'm trying to think. Give me a drink.

*He fetches the wine bottle and a glass.*

Come on! Come on!

*He pours her a glass and she gulps it down. She holds out the glass for more.*

**John**    You've had enough.

**Julie**    No such thing. POUR.

*He does so.*

God I want a cigarette, where the hell are Christine's?

**John**    No idea.

**Julie**    I don't regret anything. Everything's just dandy. I'll run away just like the pictures –

**John**    Miss Julie –

**Julie**    Shut up! Have you seen that one with . . . I've lost my thought . . . did I tell you about my mother? She had this thing about women's emancipation . . . she swore she'd never marry so she told my father she would be his lover but never his wife.

*Pause.*

But then . . . I was born. I was . . . a mistake, really.

**John**    You're illegitimate?

**Julie**    Mmm, funny isn't it? So they had to get married and my mother brought me up as . . . a child of nature. She wanted me to demonstrate the equality of the sexes. She used to dress me up in boy's clothes and made me learn about farming – she made me kill a fox when I was . . .

*She pauses briefly, remembering.*

And then she reorganised the estate, the women had to do the men's work and the men the women's. We were the laughing stock of the whole county. Finally, my father snapped and she fell into line. But she began to stay out all night . . . she took lovers, people talked, she blamed my father for the failure of her experiment . . . her infidelities were her revenge. They rowed constantly, and fought, she often had terrible gashes and bruises . . . he did too, she was very strong when she was angry . . . and then there was a rumour that my father tried to kill himself . . .

*John is stunned.*

Yes, he failed . . . (*smiles*) obviously.

*Pause.*

I didn't know whose side I was on . . . I think I learnt all my emotions by the age of ten and never developed any more. A child experiences the world so deeply . . . without the sophistication to protect itself . . . it's not fair really.

*Pause.*

My mother – almost on her deathbed – no, *on* her deathbed, made me swear that I'd never be a slave to any man.

**John**   And the Officer?

**Julie**   He was to be *my* slave.

**John**   But he did a runner.

**Julie**   It was more complicated than that.

**John**   Didn't look like it.

**Julie**   From your vantage point probably not. How can *you* see? You watch the world through eyes filled with acid.

**John**   You hate me too?

**Julie**   Of course.

**John**   But not when I was inside you.

**Julie**   I was weak, I won't be again. If it were up to me I'd have you shot, like a fallen horse at the Grand National and fed to the dogs.

**John**   Only thoroughbreds run the National.

**Julie**   They let the odd nag in, ones with weak chests, '*pour encourager les autres.*'

*He grabs hold of her and forces her down on the table, head first.*

You wouldn't dare!

*He pulls up her dress.*

Supposing your sow squeals for her pig? Supposing Daddy rings his bell?

*He lets her go.*

The truth is, I must bolt. Enjoy myself for a couple of days, a week if I can stand myself that long and then . . .

*She gestures across her throat, unseen by him.*

**John**   New York sounds more attractive.

**Julie**   You?! In the capital of the world?! You wouldn't survive five minutes! You, with your clumsy hands and grubby nails, your quick wit but slow, slow mind. Your pub talk and your pools and the way you swill your beer like a mouthwash. You wouldn't suit New York – in your ill-fitting suit – your demob disaster – hacked together by some gnarled troll in the East End. You? Run a nightclub? I remember you at the village fair, you couldn't even run the egg-and-spoon race because of your 'weak chest'!

**John**   At last, the true blue blood speaks! The little blue-blooded bastard! And you called *me* a snob? I read up on your 'pedigree' once, that book in your father's study (*glances up*). Would you like to know who your earliest ancestor was? A farmer, a stinking, stupid farmer and five hundred years ago he pimped his wife to the king. And in return . . . all this. Doubtless she enjoyed it, the slag. The blood of a whore runs through you for centuries.

*He holds her face. They stare at each other.*

**Julie**   Die with me John, a suicide pact.

**John**   Suicide's for cowards.

**Julie**   Chicken.

**John**   It's a crime against God's law.

**Julie**   You believe in God?

**John**   Passionately. I'm in love with the bloke.

*He breaks free of her.*

I'm going to bed.

*He starts to exit.*

**Julie**   You forget who I am.

*He stops.*

**John**   Oh yeah, sorry.

*He takes some loose change from his pocket and throws it on the table.*

**John**   Here's a few bob. Cheers, darling.

**Julie** (*calm*)   Not enough. You take my virginity, you humiliate me, you abuse me and my family's honour – there's a *price*. You don't leave this room. You listen to what I say or help me God I will scream rape and I will not stop screaming until you are in prison.

**John**   Miss Julie . . . I'm sorry. I'm sorry I've hurt you. I know you're suffering, I'm sorry for that, truly. But I'm to be married. This is where I belong and so do you. In time you'll forget about this until it's just a dull ache. You'll live with it, that's life.

**Julie**   Pain hurts, I won't tolerate it.

**John**   You have to.

*Pause.*

**Julie**   Why don't you love me?

**John**   I do.

**Julie**   No. Why *can't* you love me?

*Pause.*

**John**  Fear.

*Pause.*

**Julie**  John . . . tell me what to do. Order me. I'm so tired I can't think. My legs feel hollowed out, as if I've no blood.

**John**  Go upstairs. Get dressed. Get money for the journey – from your father's desk, second drawer down, the key's on the mantelpiece under the clock.

**Julie**  Come with me.

**John**  I can't.

**Julie**  No, to my room.

*He hesitates.*

**John**  I can't.

**Julie**  Please.

**John**  Go. Come down when you're ready, I'll drive you to the station.

**Julie**  Be nice to me.

**John**  Orders never sound nice. Now you know. *Go.*

*She exits.*

**John** *opens the shutters and begins to 'normalise' the room: he pockets his change, bins the dog medicine, hides the clutch bag, empties the ashtray, clears the bottle and glass, removes the rag from the bin and manages to slip it into his pocket as* **Christine** *enters.*

*She's dressed for church. She carries a suit, shirt and tie on a hanger.*

**Christine**  Morning.

**John**  Morning, love.

**Christine**  I gave these a press, for church.

*She hands him his clothes.*

**John**  Cheers. Won't be a minute.

*He goes to exit.*

**Christine**    No one's up, get dressed in here.

**John**    In here?

**Christine**    Hurry up, we'll be late.

*He starts to get changed.* **Christine** *sits and observes him. Silence.*

**John**    What's the lesson today?

**Christine**    I don't know. You look tired.

**John**    Nightmares, the usual. You slept all right?

**Christine**    Like a log.

*He's struggling with his tie a little.*

**John**    Will you do this?

*She ties his tie. He strokes her cheek. She catches his hand and smells his fingers.*

**Christine**    These need a wash.

*They look at each other. Suddenly she slaps him hard on the cheek. He stares at her.*

**Christine**    I woke in the night, I opened your door.

*Pause.*

You both had your backs to me.

*Pause.*

I was wondering if you'd tell me, since we are to be married, for better or worse.

**John**    'Course I'd've told you. I'm sorry.

**Christine**    Don't bother. I imagine you did it with every little scrubber in France. I have low expectations, I'm rarely disappointed. I understand, how could you resist her beauty when you're just a man?

*She slaps him again.*

We're not staying here by the way, so you can forget it ever happening again. I'm not working in a house where I can't respect my superiors.

**John**    There's more to life than respecting superiors.

**Christine**    You hypocrite, you cringe before his Lordship. I've seen you; reading his books, trying to engage him in 'political conversation'. You bore him, he thinks you're a crawler.

*Beat.*

I'm surprised at her though, had it been a gentleman, I could understand it, but *you* . . . who are you?

**John**    It wasn't her fault, I took advantage.

**Christine**    Ah, defending his mistress's honour, how noble.

*Pause.*

What was she like?

**John**    Christine –

**Christine**    No, don't tell me, I saw.

*Beat.*

Your rash is getting worse.

*Beat.*

Look at you, you can't believe it, can you? You're still reliving it in your head, your dirty little film in your dirty little fleapit of a mind.

**John**    You've made your point.

**Christine**    We'll hand in our notice today. We'll go to Leeds. We'll stay with my sister while we get sorted. You can find work as a porter or a caretaker. Somewhere steady and secure with a good pension for a wife. And children.

We'll be wanting to start a family as soon as we're married. Won't we?

**John**   Yes.

*A door slams overhead in the study.*

**Christine**   Who's that?

**John**   Claire, probably.

**Christine**   Could it be his Lordship? Home early? He might've got the first train?

**John**   No, he'd have telephoned.

**Christine**   Well, he might be about to – have you done his shoes?

**John**   Nearly.

**Christine**   I'll make his coffee.

**John**   I'll do it. You don't want to be late for church, I'll catch you up on the way. Go on . . . it's fine . . . I'll serve him his coffee, have a shave and then . . .

**Christine**   What?

*He can't speak. He's decided to run away with* **Miss Julie**.

What?

**John**   I've just got things . . . to do.

**Christine**   Fine. I'll wait for you at the gate.

**John**   The gate.

**Christine**   At the end of the drive.

**John**   I know.

**Christine** *exits.* **John** *paces, working it out, excited.*

*After a while,* **Miss Julie** *enters dressed to travel. She carries a suitcase, bag, hatbox and a birdcage covered with a cloth.* **John** *helps her.*

**Julie**   I saw Christine going out.

**John**   She's off to church.

*He gazes at her.*

**Julie**   Does she suspect?

**John**   No, nothing. You look . . . so beautiful.

**Julie**   Do I?

**John**   Yes.

*She opens her case and takes out a child's white dress with a pink ribbon.*

**Julie**   Look. My dress. It was in the nursery.

*She holds it against herself. He caresses her.*

**Julie**   Come with me. There was a fortune in Daddy's desk. Come with me, wherever you want, don't leave me alone.

**John**   Show me.

**Julie**   It's in my bag.

*He takes out a huge wad of notes. Stares at them in amazement.*

**John**   It would take me five years to earn this.

*Pause.*

Fine. Let's go. But *now*!

**Julie**   I'm ready!

*He puts on his jacket, she helps him.*

**John**   We have to go now!

**Julie**   I'm ready! You haven't got any shoes on!

**John**   I'll get some.

*She gestures to her father's shoes.*

**Julie**   Wear those.

*He hesitates. She insists now.*

Put them on . . .

*He hesitates.*

Put them on, John.

*He thinks then puts them on, she watches him intently.*

**John**   And no luggage, it's a giveaway.

**Julie**   Yes, only what we can take in the compartment.

*He notices the birdcage.*

**John**   What's that?

*She removes the cloth.*

**Julie**   It's Serena, she's mine. I can't leave her here.

**John**   Don't be ridiculous, we can't take that!

**Julie**   Don't be cruel, let me take her!

**John**   Put it down. Put the cage down! Put – the cage – down!

**Julie**   DON'T ORDER ME!

**John**   Shh! Your father might be back any minute – Christine – anyone. Give me the cage.

**Julie**   I'm not leaving her here. Let's set her free.

**John**   It's a house bird, it wouldn't survive a day out there.

**Julie**   Then kill her.

*Pause.*

Are you scared?

**John**   No.

*She takes the bird out of the cage.*

**Julie**   Please don't let her suffer.

*She stares at the bird.*

Must you die and leave your mistress behind?

*She gives John the bird. He takes it over to the chopping block.*

**John**   Please, no scenes. It's a dumb animal. I'm going to kill it and then we'll go . . . understand . . . I suggest you look away . . . UNDERSTAND.

*She nods. He looks around for the hatchet. She hands him the bread knife.*

*He looks away. She stares, transfixed.*

**Julie** (*quietly*)   Don't . . .

*He cuts the bird's head off.*

*He wipes the blade on a rag.*

There's blood between us.

**John**   Let's go.

**Julie**   Go? With you? Now?

*She picks up the decapitated bird and smears blood from it onto his face.*

Who's scared of blood? Who's scared of blood? Tell me, who's scared of blood?

*She kisses him aggressively then thrusts her hand into his trousers.*

How much would this bleed? Would it bleed like me . . . like last night . . . ? I could use your skull to drink from . . . open you up like a carcass and climb inside you . . . thrash about in your weak, wet chest . . . roast your heart with my breath and eat it whole. You think I'm weak? Because I wanted you inside me? It's just biology – just chemicals – you think I want to run away with you and carry your brats in my body . . . feed your spawn with my blood . . . you've got another thing coming Mister . . . come on! You think I want your child? You think I want to take your name? Look at me . . . what *is* your name? Your surname? I've never heard it . . .

maybe you haven't got one? I'd be Mrs Scum, Mrs Barrow
Boy . . . mmm? Is that what you want? A nice little wife? A
nice girl like me? You dog who wears my crest upon your
buttons. That's what you are! Buttons. You think I'd share
you with my cook? *Come on* . . . aren't you having fun ?

*She removes her hand and sits at the table.*

Daddy will be home soon, he finds his desk open, second
drawer down, his money gone. He rings on the bell – twice
for his lackey – that's *you* – and then he sends for the police.
And I say it was HIM officer. (*cockney*) 'He's the one what did
it'. And I tell them everything. And then Daddy has a heart
attack and drops down dead. End of the line. The train will
terminate at this station. The bloodline clots. No heirs. No
more of us. Dead. But what of the lackey? Oh, that'll be the
pauper's line, third stop after the gutter, it ends in jail.

*Enter* **Christine**. *She stands in the doorway.*

And here's the mother. 'Got a fag, ducks?'

**Christine** *surveys the scene: the suitcase, the dead bird, the cash, the
dress, the blood on* **John***'s face.*

*She produces a cut-throat razor from her bag.*

**Christine** (*measured*)   I remembered at the gate; your
razor's broke. You couldn't shave. You can now. I
borrowed this from the gatekeeper.

**Julie**   His dog screwed my dog.

**Christine** *hands* **John** *the razor.*

**Christine**   Go and shave. We're late for church.

**John** *exits.*

**Julie**   Christine, you're my friend, we've always had our
little chats, haven't we? Listen –

**Christine**   Where were you going?

**Julie** New York. Not my idea, but if you listen . . . oh you're angry . . . listen: me and John . . . we're in love with each other –

**Christine** I don't want to know.

**Julie** You see we simply can't stay here and –

**Christine** He's not going anywhere.

**Julie** (*snaps*) Please try to be calm, Christine!

*Beat.*

It's a very nice name, Christine. So we can't stay here for various reasons too complicated to go into but I've had this brilliant idea which is that all three of us go to New York together and we open a nightclub . . . I've got some money, you see . . . you mustn't tell anyone I stole it . . . and me and John would run it and you could be in charge of the kitchen. Wouldn't that be nice? Do say yes because if you say yes then everything'll be nice and not dreadful. Oh, can I have one?

**Christine** *gives* **Miss Julie** *a cigarette and a light.*

**Julie** Thank you. You'd love New York . . . The Metropolitan . . . that's a museum and The Empire State Building which is so high that when you're at the top the people on the street look like insects . . . you're not allowed to drop a coin on them because it kills them . . . and in the winter the children skate on the lake in Central Park, when I was there with my father I skated . . . he made me . . .

*She pauses, remembering something.*

And I'm sure the nightclub will be a terrific success and there'll be dancing and we'll drink whenever we want because we'll own all the drink . . . and with your looks, I'm not flattering or patronising you, you'll meet a nice husband, a rich American, you'll see . . . the Americans are charmed by us . . . they die for the accent . . . and we'll live on the Upper . . . East Side . . . or West Side . . . East or

West . . . it doesn't matter really . . . or we can always come home again . . . back here . . . or somewhere else . . . don't you think ?

**Christine**    You believe all this?

**Julie**    No.

**John** *appears, the razor in his hand.*

**Christine**    So you were going to run away. You're as mad as she is.

*He hands her the razor.*

**John**    Show some respect, she's still your mistress.

**Christine**    What *this*?!

*She points at* **Miss Julie***.*

This puddle! This is what comes of moral weakness.

*She puts the razor down.*

**John**    And you're superior? She slept with me, so did you, where's the difference?

**Christine**    Listen to him, cock of the walk! I've never sunk as low as her. Or you. I'm not a thief.

**John**    You stupid bitch! The whole war you traded on the black market, what's that, good honest toil?

**Christine**    I'm going to church.

**John**    That's right, you cling to your superstition.

**Christine**    Our saviour suffered and died on the cross for all our sins and if we approach him in faith and with a penitent heart, he will take all our sins upon him.

**John**    Including backhanders to the butcher?

**Christine** *picks up the wad of notes and puts them in her bag. Then she takes the car keys from the cupboard.*

**Christine**   And I'll take these in case anyone was thinking of leaving before his Lordship gets home.

*She exits. Silence.*

**John**   Christ, I despise religion.

**Julie**   So why practise it? Class is your religion.

**Miss Julie** *toys with the razor.* **John** *takes it from her.*

**John**   Don't do that, you'll hurt yourself.

**Julie**   I want to.

**John**   No you don't.

**Julie**   I do but I can't. Just like my father – he should've done it. The coward.

**John**   You're tired.

**Julie**   Shattered.

**John**   You want some tea?

**Julie**   No thanks.

**John**   I'm having some . . .

**Julie**   No.

*He puts the kettle on. She picks up the razor again.*

She didn't leave any cigarettes did she?

**John**   What do you think?

*Pause.*

Your father's not a coward.

**Julie**   Oh, he is.

*She toys with the razor.*

You don't know him. You don't know what it's like to be Daddy's special girl. Of course I love him, I love him as much as I hate him. He's inside my head all the time. And my mother. Who's to blame for what we are? It's a horrible, ugly mess. My thoughts are his, my feelings are hers. An endless circle.

**John**   Circles are always endless.

*The bell rings. Three sharp rings, loud.*

Your father's back!

*He rushes to the phone, instinctively straightening his tie.*

**John** (*in phone*)   This is John, sir . . . Yes, sir . . . Yes, sir . . . Yes, sir.

**Julie**   Three bags full, sir.

**John**   Very good, sir . . . excellent party, sir . . . no not too much drinking, sir . . . thank you, sir . . . yes, everyone had an excellent time, sir. No, no damage, sir . . . Yes, right away.

*He puts the phone down.*

(*panicking*) He wants his shoes and his coffee immediately!

*He looks for the shoes on the table. Gone. Then, horrified, he remembers he's wearing them. He pulls them off and puts them on the table.*

Give these a once over will you? (*He stops, suddenly.*) Sorry.

**Julie**   You thought I was her?

**John**   Yes, forgive me.

**Julie** (*to herself*)   It was nice.

**John** *runs around, preparing: he fetches a coffee pot, china crockery and a silver tray. He polishes a teaspoon and then starts grinding coffee beans.*

**Miss Julie** *watches him, appalled at his servitude.*

**Julie**   Look at you . . . grinding away . . . so loyal . . . John The Baptist. And daddy is . . . Herod. And I am Salome.

**John**   You're still drunk.

*She approaches him with the razor, preventing his work.*

**Julie**   I am Salome and you can have your revenge, John.
Give the order. You know I can take orders. What does
killing feel like, tell me how it feels.

*She strokes his cheek with the razor.*

**John**   It feels like nothing. You obey the order.

**Julie**   Give the order, Officer.

**John**   I'm not an Officer.

*He grips her wrist to prevent her slashing him or herself. They move
together slowly. A strange dance.*

**Julie**   I know, it's not fair, is it? Give the order – deserter –
boy – peasant. Order me.

*Beat.*

What would you do if Daddy rang his bell and ordered you
to cut your throat? You'd obey, wouldn't you . . . because
you must . . . because you were born to obey. Give the
order, slave.

**John**   Do it yourself.

**Julie**   No fun on my own. Order me. Be the hypnotist at
the village fair. You remember the fair. I saw you there that
last summer, before the war . . . remember?

*He nods.*

You saw me . . . that's when I knew you wanted me, you
were chained to Christine . . . already buried alive . . . but I
know you saw me . . . you were hypnotised . . . describe my
dress.

**John**   White with a pink ribbon . . .

**Julie**   Here . . .

*She gestures across her throat with the razor. He gently takes it from
her.*

And you looked at me as we queued for the hypnotist, you looked at me with longing, you looked at the one who had everything and you stepped aside, you said, 'After you, Miss Julie'.

**John**   You smiled, you said:

**Julie**   Thank you, John.

**John**   How did you know my name?

**Julie**   Because I asked my father.

**John**   Why?

**Julie**   Because I wanted you. Because I'd felt your eyes upon me forever . . . because you do my father's dirty work . . . because you've always been watching me, waiting for me . . . because you want revenge . . . my father's angel with your eyes upon me forever.

*Pause.*

And the hypnotist says to his subject . . . 'Take this broom' and you feel that there's a broom in your hand and you take the broom and he says 'Sweep' and you sweep and afterwards you remember nothing.

**John**   You have to be asleep first.

**Julie**   I am asleep. The room is filled with smoke and you're an iron stove, you're a man dressed in black with a top hat, your eyes glow like coals when the fire dies and your face is white as ash.

*He eases the razor into her hand.*

**John**   Here's the broom . . .

*He whispers in her ear.*

*She turns to him, holding the razor, she nods.*

*They kiss briefly, tenderly.*

*As they slowly part the bell rings, once, loud.*

*He starts, she holds him.*

**Julie**    It's only a bell. Pray for me . . .

**John**    I don't believe in God.

**Julie**    But pray for me.

*The bell rings again, twice.*

It's just a bell, my darling angel . . .

**John**    It's not just a bell. There's someone behind it. And a hand that sets it in motion . . . and a vast spinning universe that sets the hand in motion. And if you stop your ears it rings louder until you answer, until the police come . . . it's hell . . . and there's nothing else . . . *go.*

**Miss Julie** *walks to the door, the razor in her hand, she doesn't look back.*

*She exits.*

**John** *sits at the table.*

*He starts to polish the shoes.*

*Twenty seconds.*

*Blackout.*